DAYLIGHT OF SEAGULLS
Alice Allen

Alice Allen was born in London and grew up in Jersey in the Channel Islands. She lives in the UK with her husband and two children. Alice has an MPhil in Creative Writing from the University of South Wales and a degree in English from Cambridge University. Alice is published in several literary magazines and anthologies and in 2014 won the Flambard Poetry Prize.

DAYLIGHT OF SEAGULLS

Alice Allen

Alice Allen

From your cousin Alice
x

The High Window

First published in the UK in 2019 by The High Window Press
3 Grovely Close
Peatmoor
Swindon
SN5 5SN
Email: abbeygatebooks@yahoo.co.uk

Designed and typeset in Palatino Linotype
by The High Window Press.
Cover image, *Seagulls On Wall,* by Claude Cahun, reproduced with permission of Jersey Heritage Collections © Jersey Heritage
Photograph of Alice Allen on back cover © A.Griffiths 2019
Printed and bound by Lulu.com.

ArtHouseJersey
Supported by ArtHouse Jersey

For my family
and
in memory of Eve and Richard Allen

CONTENTS

Suppose I make a time piece of humanity
Demonstrate the movement of the century hand –
Will war not wither like an unused letter, drop
From your alphabet, vanish from our little gap
Of time?

Velimir Khlebnikov
28 January 1922

trans. Paul Schmidt

Introduction

The island my mother grew up in during the 1940s was one of small farms and fishing communities, where many spoke Jèrriais, an old form of Norman French with Norse, Breton and Medieval Latin influences. As in the other Channel Islands, the native inhabitants of Jersey possessed French-sounding surnames and, although proudly British, had a distinctive cuisine and many customs that were similar to those found in nearby Normandy and Brittany in France. Channel Islanders would drink English tea but might have it with a slice of Guernsey *gâche* (an enriched fruit bread), or at Easter time with several *merveilles* or 'wonders' (a twisted raised pastry a little like a dainty doughnut).

In June 1940 Jersey, Guernsey, Alderney and the other, smaller Channel Islands were occupied by Nazi Germany for nearly five years. The invasion brought with it, as it did to other occupied countries in Europe, widespread restrictions on almost every aspect of people's daily lives and, towards the end, near starvation. It also brought contact with people from other countries, on a scale not experienced by islanders before. Thousands of civilians and prisoners of war were brought to the islands from all over Europe, the Soviet Union and North Africa to work as forced and slave labour, building the walls, gun emplacements, tunnels and bunkers that would make the Channel Islands one of the most fortified places in occupied Europe.

The Channel Islanders' experience of occupation was radically different to the British war experience. It has never held a place within Britain's heroic World War II narrative.

Growing up in Jersey during the 1970s and '80s we weren't taught about the Occupation (as it is known in the Channel Islands, with a capital 'O') at school apart from perhaps a passing mention of the food shortages and ingenious ways of making coffee out of parsnips. The more extreme traumas of that time were not mentioned: the brutal treatment of the forced labourers, the fate of the Jewish population and the islanders who defied or resisted the Nazis.

But from an early age I was aware of that time as a constant presence in the minds of those members of my family who were children during the Occupation. A child myself, I was fascinated by their 'child's-eye' view of war. I was happy to move with the tide of their recurring stories and memories that would be told many times over, their minds seeming to work away at something that couldn't be solved or resolved.

Now, people discuss the Occupation more openly. There are many history books, academic studies, museums and memorials as well as published personal memoirs and diaries that bear testament to the suffering that was once overlooked in the official narratives.

GERS EY

Geirr's Island –
Norse man, naming this land his own.
From L'Etacq to Le Hocq the coastline
is a fan, a flame of brandished rock
doubling at low tide. Each rock named –
etchièrviéthe, marmotchiéthe, sablionniéthe –
the language of rock prodding and poking
the coast over time – from Ick Hoc
to Hygge Hogge, to Hic Hoc, to Icho Isle
with an imprint of witch.

In sun the rocks graze brown to pink
to *souothè*. Encircled by the sea's salt suck
they hunch and fret like something spilt, burnt
and set. There are eyes in the rock
where sea can pass. *Souachehouais*
in the rock where sea can swash.

From north to south the island
is a wedge, tapering out
to little coves and open dunes,
sea spray, spindrift, sand-glitter, gloss,
down to the harbour with its *scoucherels*,
its reek of shell and flesh and salt,
down to the busy granite town,
people going about their day,
pebbles rolling on the tide.

etchièrviéthe rock frequented by cormorants; *marmotchiéthe* murmuring
rock; *sablionniéthe* sandy rock; *souothè* yellowish brown, sorel-coloured;
souachehouais swashway; *scoucherel* skulking place

STRANGELY DIFFERENT

April 1940, States of Jersey tourism leaflet

Happily
our island is far removed
from the theatre of war.

The bays
with their eternal sands
sea and sunshine
produce an atmosphere

of peace
strangely different
from the rest of the world.

Holiday camps
boarding houses
hotels with ballrooms.

Travel by steamer.

Banish the spectre of war
from your mind.

A SAPPER'S TALE

The evacuation of British troops from St Malo, June 1940

Then orders came to retreat –
it took two hours to creep into St Malo,
the roads messy with our soldiers and tanks.
French civilians were heading south,
mattresses strapped to their car rooves,
barrows and carts filled with blankets and pans.

Fires burned in the fields –
our lot had bonfired their supplies
before getting into enemy hands.

An aeroplane flew overhead, one of ours.
They waved to us and I thought, lucky blighters,
you'll be having breakfast in England.

Redcaps tried to retain order but stragglers
disappeared through gates in the walled city,
down narrow cobbled streets
looking for a last drink.
Some were left behind –
got a shock when they sobered up.

By afternoon we were lined up on the dock.
A hotchpotch fleet of civvy boats was there to meet us,
like at Dunkirk, but these were from Jersey,
potato boats, fishing vessels, handsome leisure yachts,
steered by teenagers and old men.

An ancient channel ferry took me home
but the smaller boats stayed for our demolition boys
blowing up the lock gates to the harbour.
They all got away just as German soldiers
reached the battlement walls of the deserted city.

PORTICO GLASS

While the adults dug potatoes,
we were playing houses
in the foyer of the field
(mine had two rooms,
marked out with sticks,
a potato crate door)
when Poppa called all of us
into the house, and we waited
with our gas masks on.
Mummy nursed the baby
on a wicker chair,
a wet cloth over his face,
too small for a mask.

Amateurs, we gathered
in the hallway
as if waiting for visitors,
(not sheltering under tables
or the stairs) and prayed,
me and my sister,
in the light of the gumdrop-coloured
Victorian glass which would have
shattered, blinding us,
had the bombs hit.

WHATEVER ELSE IS WRONG, IT'S BEEN A BEAUTIFUL DAY

It began with a hush –
        lines of Tommies,
sailors, airmen
returning to the Mainland
like the outgoing tide.

Sticky queues of labelled children,
triple dressed and barley-sugared,
waiting for the mail boat,
the coal boat, the next boat out.

Falling from the sky in a canvas pouch,
the General's Ultimatum,
red ribbons streaming,
summoning white flags.

Remember Old Touzel
rigging up his underpants
from a chimney pot?

Bombers came
while farmers unloaded
tomatoes, potatoes
down at the St Helier quay.

And high up in his plane
the Luftwaffe boy
sees wave crest, glass house,
harbour and bay.

Cows grazing on the airfield.

How pleasing to take in
all of a place in one blink.
How easily taken.

LA SOUPE D'ANDGULLE

The man who brings the *vraic*
also brings conger eel
flung into a loop on top of the basket,
cheaper than the market eels
dressed and curled on a silver plate,
the heavy tips of their tails stuffed
inside their mouths like a warning.

The unglistening eel is dead
but only just. Being the eldest girl,
Dulcie's job is to hold it straight
as Maman puts the apron on ready to gut;
its freshness flinches under the blunt knife,
an oily questing still present in the cells,
the refusal of its body to understand.
They say a conger eel
can swim backwards if pressed.

Maman is swift to make the eel listen,
working the flesh into clean steaks;
her swollen washday hands
turn agile and particular
in the presence of this fish,
placing pieces into the pot, basting, no,
anointing the eel in its juices,
the milk-sweet fragrance of the stock,
a scattering of parsley and marigold petals.

Now Dulcie stands on Margate Pier
two weeks since evacuation,
living with a relative she doesn't know,
looking at pots of jellied eels,
grey, congealed thumbs, in disbelief.

vraic seaweed

19

A SEA FOG

delicate and tasty
tunnels through the lanes,
resting in the hedges
on the elms' tight branches
filling up the fields.

A full, articulate fog –
droplets formed around
a nucleus of salt.

Out of this pink hover
a child pedals down the lane
on hose-pipe tyres,
a forbidden news-sheet
in a pouch under her blouse,
an empty bottle in her basket.

Three times a week her parents
shush her off to Mrs Clegg's.
Milk for news. News for milk.

The bike is cumbersome
but on the way home
there are trinkets to find
in the half-hidden hedges,
the crumbling mud banks

and she whispers their shapes to me
now with her stiff wrinkled fingers:
pennywort, shale rock,
a play ball of moss.

EMPTYING THE EGG OF ITS SONG

In those days   I'd go collecting
all seven years of me up a tree
the sweet stink of my fingers
prising for a nest
I'd bring the eggs down in my mouth
    blackbird   sparrow   tit
Common birds   nothing fancy
Marbles on my tongue

One nest in particular
                    a wren's
made from green leaf and feather
a freshness   spun into a dome
of dainty wickerwork I had to break
to find the speckled eggs
five of them   mine

I'd be home before curfew
blowing them by the stove
a sleek sack of goo
hitting the saucer   shell intact
A quietness following after

Curfew   the word itself was like a bird
bringing the night in its beak
Sometimes we'd hear the soldiers
firing in the moonlight
on manoeuvres
marching down our lane

And when that last siege winter comes
I lie in bed hungry as a stone
the covers so cold they feel wet
as if all the woodland streams
run through the room
and cup around the bed

and I fall asleep   on pebbles and lichen
feathers and hay
    and the water carrying us all
    soldier   boy   bird
    I don't know where away

BEEHIVE STORES

'I beg to declare I have a small grocer shop…
a Jewish Undertaking poster is on the window'
                    Letter, 22 November 1940

Hyam Goldman worries about his bees.
They might die from gunfire shock
as it clatters through the valley,

or soldiers on creeping knees
might come at night
and steal the hives away.

The shop sells tinned goods,
balls of string, dried beans,
honey.

Elderly, dressed in white
with smoker and veil,
he checks the frames.

Here is food, here is medicine
for wound and burn.
Candlelight.

The bees pin flight paths
through the valley sleeves
of chestnut, oak and sycamore,

through sweet garden pockets
and hollow-lane hedges,
stopping to sip at pools in the earth.

Listen to the sound
a hive makes
remembering, remembering.

Stock: £10 17s 6d
notes the administrator
for Aryanisation.

Each hive
an anxious box
of productivity.

Each bee
a barrel
filled with sun.

IDENTITY CARD

Jersey Archive, St Helier

January 1941. They have walked the half mile to the Parish Hall in a squall of rain to have their photographs taken. My grandmother has left her farmyard coverall at home and wears a heavy coat, a white wool shawl pinned at her throat with a brooch. My grandfather wears a face I don't recognise, a shocked uncertainty at something in the distance. He doesn't have time to understand; they must get home to bring the cows in.

The whole island will be registered this way. Name, address, date and place of birth. Some of the cards will be marked in red with a J.

Later, a clerk will gather together the paperwork, like local clerks all over Europe, forwarding it on to the Nazi administration with, "I beg to report" and "I have the honour to enclose".

The new year has brought a particularly cold snap. Everyone has made an effort to wrap up. You can sense the winter damp in their clothes, the peaty tweed coats, gaberdines, the too-tight shabby jackets, hand-knitted mufflers speckled with dropped stitches. There is a sprig of wintersweet in the beekeeper's lapel.

TRENCH

Five children look out of the window at the front field. Two
workers are digging a trench under guard. The workers do not
look right. They have sacking tied where shoes should be. There
are holes and rips in their clothes. The children can tell just by
looking that they smell dirty. When the guard wanders off, the
workers stop digging and walk, very slowly, to the door of the
farmhouse. They hold out their hands. The mother gives them
each a cold boiled potato, the skin lifting off in grey quarters. The
workers kiss the back of her hand. She is strange with fear. They
eat in a hurry and walk back to the field. The next morning the
children are back at the window. The workers are back at the
trench. One of the men falls out of sight. The guard is lifting a
chouque high above his head. The five children do not know what
to do with what they see. Come away, come away, come away.
Adults now, the children look out from the window and tell their
story, surprised at how easily it unfolds. Surprised at how they do
not know what to do with what they have seen.

chouque a heavy wooden stick, a club

26

FOREIGN WORKER

Atlantic Wall, St Ouen's Bay, Jersey

After Günter Eich

This is his cap
made from a sack.

This is his shirt,
a blanket.

This is his belt,
clothes-hanger wire.

This is his coat,
a girl's jacket.

These are his shoes,
bags tied with string.

This is his skin,
stiff with cement

and swollen over the bones
of his tumbling face.

These are his eyes.
Meet them.

ARRIVAL OF THE SLAVE WORKERS

Diary entries, 13-15 August 1942

No sun today
        went to town
hundreds of Russians
        men and boys
so far from
        witness today
barefooted boys
        dressed in rags
pitiful sight
        so far from
put in those camps
        none were soldiers
whips and truncheons
        so far from
witness today
        some were women
few had shoes
        more arrive
men of seventy
        so far from
from Ukraine
        none of them soldiers
a sorry state
        a lady's blouse
witness today
        more arrive
so far from
        how can how can
pitiful sight
        so far from
home

POTATO, FLOUR

She is peeling potatoes when he comes,
a shadow at the side window,
a wingbeat on the edge of her vision.
She clicks the latch on the door.
There he stands, stooping a little
to meet her height. Hand
gestures to mouth – he is starving.
A plate of left-over porridge, an apple.
He eats, bows his head and is gone.

She is boiling potatoes when they come,
two boys at the window, barely fourteen.
She clicks the latch on the door.
There they stand. One has no shoes,
his feet bleeding. Hands gesture to mouths –
they are starving. Two plates of boiled potatoes,
a pair of broken shoes with wooden soles.

She is drying potato flour when he comes,
trays of starchy dust laid out on the sill.
He waits at the door while she clicks the latch.
Cold porridge, an onion is all that she can…
Russe, Russe, he gestures to himself.
English, she says. He laughs and claps.
Same, same, he says, then eats – he is starving.
He kisses her hand, hears the guard shouting,
bows his head and is gone.

THE SAND-GATHERING RAILWAY

No ghosts, but an imprint of sadness
is pressed onto this coastline,
close as layers of sediment in rock,
like the repetition of hard labour,

the sound of sand shovelling
onto the wagon decks,
ticker-ticker thud of locomotives
disappearing round the bay.

The railway was laid on dunes,
track and sleepers fastened with dogspikes
to defy the fidgety sand. Extra cables
pinned it down on a spring tide.

The sand here in the east of the island is sharp,
each grain of quartz a fist of edges
fractured by the worrying nature of the sea,
perfect for concrete.

Look closely, you can see glitter
in every wall and bunker, tunnel, tower,
batterie and gun-pit made by forced hand –
should any of those men return they'd find

a car park with the footprint
of a mound of stockpiled sand,
threads of hoggin road across the common,
a pier post in the layby near the ice-cream van.

From time to time a dogspike
rises to the surface of the golf course.

NO HINTERLAND
Alderney, Channel Islands

In the skull there are rocky places
and places of light.

The men work into the ground.

This island with bite-shape coves
and rainbow *vraic*.

The wind blew them down
and they didn't get up.

This island with pink sea fans
and velvet swimming crabs.

See, the body swells before death.

Who saw who saw
buried at the sea shore
        fifty feet beyond the harbour wall.

This island with orchid wings
and spinning-top shells.

A boy dying on a bed of straw and lice
Maman, Maman.

The soul flies out of its socket.

On this island without trees
you have to burn the front doors.

The men work into the ground.
And the women?

Eating grass, eating flowers, raw potato.

Who saw who saw
buried at the sea shore

and the sea to-ing and fro-ing
dragging a wrinkled carpet over the floor.

In the rock pools and the whirlpools
in the wave prints on the wet sands
in the cavelets on the mine beds.

Who saw who saw
no hinterland, no walking east

sea lavender

vraic seaweed

SOAP HOARD

In cupboards and chests, in flower boxes underneath the bed, we found soaps – seventy-eight of them – when she died. Never wanting to be without again. Each one unused.

I will not list all the scents and shapes except to say each one was pleasing to hold in the palm, naked and smooth, or wrapped in waxy tissue paper, pleated like a pouffe. I had given her the lemon ones.

And pressed into an envelope we found one that had been used, a cloudy lens of Occupation soap made at the piggery, the remnant of a tablet she had bartered for at the door with a Spanish labourer.

I see them together at dusk, standing on the threshold.

She, a farmer's wife, shouting at her children in Jèrriais. *Tais ta becque! Tais ta becque!* He, a forced labourer in a black bowler hat.

They are standing in the shadows, as strange to one another as tallow and ash.

tais ta becque be quiet

TINS AND JARS

I thought nothing of it as a child,
my grandparents' overstocked cupboard,
packets of lentils, bags of beans,
enough tins to build the finest
grocer's ziggurat.

My family's drive to forage
long before it was fashionable –
parties of us snatching razor fish
from sandy keyholes at low tide,
scabbing for winkles on the craggiest rocks,
wild sorrel delved from the hedge.

Survival food, fetched home and prepared
with ceremony and grace,
revered at a table once set
on the outer ripple
of an engineered famine –

bracken soup, carrageen moss,
echoes of a blockade,
limpets, acorns. *Let 'em starve.*

I too make the family recipe,
with my glut of green tomatoes –
a savoury jam that never sets,
the rust-red jars
glowing on my shelf.

LISTENING PARTY

Hidden in the teapot,
buried in the pram,
placed with the biscuits
in the Coronation tin – wireless sets –
taken out and carried to the table
with the hushed ceremony of a well-laid
afternoon tea tray.

All around the island,
from white-washed fishermen's huts
to the Bailiff's chintzed snug,
people gather in small groups:

nurses, bakers, news-sheet typists,
labourers, gravediggers,
parish church preachers

and schoolteacher Mr Le Druillenec
cycling to his sister's,
an English/Russian dictionary
in his breast pocket
for the man hiding in the attic.
He'll collect his weekly rations
from her shop, then join them,
listening to the news at nine o'clock.

OPEN DAY AT THE OBSERVATORY

'Observatory Director, Father Charles Rey points out
the epicentre of an earthquake in central Asia, at the
Maison St Louis Observatory, Jersey, 1937'
Photograph caption

i

Inside glass boxes, framed in polished wood,
instruments record the invisible:
a palm-sized stopwatch with silver penny wings
catches the wind's speed, the paper lantern cylinder
of the anemotachometer records its force,
a pendulum dangles for earthquakes on the basement floor.

It seems right, a man of religion making instruments
to capture what we cannot see. Miniature workings
measure and tick, pump and fall. A brass arm inks
a glacier on a scroll of slowly turning paper.
We climb the spiral stair to wind vanes on the roof,
the island town before us: office blocks, Waterfront,

fog coming with salt in its teeth. Strangers, we are cold up here.
What resonance are we equipped to record?

ii

The radio is part machine part miracle:
a copper coil, an earphone piece, a whisker of wire –

> *Father Charles Rey, Jesuit, Meteorologist,*
> *Keeper of the Mission's Madagascan Crystal Collection,*
> *maker of illegal listening sets for locals in the know*
> *(his own set hidden in a pocket watch)*

coaxes the signal from a fingertip of crystal,
at first a terrible scribbling nest of noise,
a miniature game of round and round
with the interference, until
the physical thrill of unmistakable
clear   human   sound

listen   how a voice can rectify the body
simultaneous   alive   found.

A SEA FOG

She wakes to a new world. The field is stuffed with fog. Since dawn it has come up from the fenced-off, mine-filled sea in drifts and streamers, passing below her window as she slept, and now it has formed one dense cloud in front of the house. Quickly and with the relish of her nine years she dresses in her knitted bathing suit and wakes her younger sister, gets her to do the same, and they skelter down the stairs while everyone else is sleeping and step out into the sea that even now is swelling in the field, and they swim like fools in its rising tide.

APPEAL

'Pregnant working women
are badly in need of baby clothes...'

People can be kind. The locals bring
mittens, booties, putty-coloured vests,
pre-war knits summoned up from a deep drawer,
the softness of a second-hand garment,
hand-made, deliberate elderly fingers
passing the wool over and under, over and under,
plain to purl to matinee jacket,
scallop-edged shawl the colour of sand.

But who are these two women
sitting, foreign, on the hospital bed?
Amused by the tiny clothes they smile their thanks
and set to, so the story goes, swaddling their babies
in torn-up strips of cotton sheet, over and under,
scooping and tucking the new-born skin –
this miraculousness – safe in their fingers,
round and round, not tied but bound the ancient way
which is a bond, which makes a bundle easy to carry
to factory or field or other working place.

If their names were known, they were not mentioned,
and what their role was here, it wasn't spoken,
except to suppose later they went back to the camp,
their babies taken from them.

THE WRECK OF THE SCHOKLAND

'The Hotel Victor Hugo was requisitioned and fitted up as a brothel, to take a considerable staff of French girls imported from Normandy... They looked what they were, a dismal line of pathetic retreads, raddled and dyed... One foggy day, they were put, all together, on a small coaster commanded by a Dutch skipper. Somewhere near Corbière it hit a rock and went down in minutes, with the loss of almost all on board. Thereafter, those of us who travelled the Island within sight of the coast, would see the girls' bodies floating offshore, sometimes several together. What caught the eye was often their long peroxide hair floating behind them, and in a peculiar way it should have been funny, but actually it was infinitely pathetic and saddening.'

A Doctor's Occupation, John Lewis

Diver

Hear the suck-hiss of my oxygen mask
as I explore her crumbling bow.
She is upright, beautiful in green water.
Her sides battered, she weighed
eleven hundred tons and sat
low – the heft of her guns.
Look! The sides of the hull
are rotten through. Light between her ribs.
There's the anchor winch, cargo winch,
stump of the mast. She was
packed with German soldiers
going home on leave,
a toilet, a bath, bags of cement
and more than thirty women
not listed on the ledger.

When the light picks through her,
chases up the stern, you can tell
she was a real steam beauty,
and I sing to her
with the suck-hiss of my mask

her-she, her-she, her-she

see – the deck planking

the jewel anemones –

her-she, her-she

a shoal of pouting

*

41

Louise

Down, down
he has lost his packet of cards
sweet soldier boy, on his way
home to mother.

Down, down
all of us falling.
The water unwraps him
hangs up his coat
unhooks his tunic.
How bright his blonde skin
now his shirt is undone.

Down, down
packed too tight in the hold
only the water can
ease us up out of the hatch.
It fills our holes
billows us into the grey.

There go his heavy boots –
my bottle of scent –

I had a brother his age

*

Dutch Relief Skipper

Fog everywhere. I couldn't see where I was going.
It was all last minute, see, flown in to cover the Captain.
Meant to be going to St Malo on a delivery and only then
returning for the passengers, but no, prancing
on the quayside with their kitbags and bright faces
in a hurry to get home, they all crammed in on board.
And me? Never been here before. I didn't know
what I was doing. I couldn't see where I was going,
and this blasted island, all reefs and rough edges
and rocks you shouldn't put there. I turned too soon,
I know it. Lucky for me I'm good at swimming.
One hundred souls dead, and all of the women.

*

Sylvie

Once on a visit to the caves
we saw steeple jacks
on the canning factory roof

lanes unravelling
towards the town

daisies and stony little paths

warm milk
in a bowl

*

Diary Writer
5, 6 and 7 January, 1943

Many small craft on the sea
searching for bodies.

One hundred passengers saved,
two hundred to be buried.

All the island's undertakers
making coffins.

Forty passengers saved,
three hundred to be buried.

Gravediggers lifting soil
in the rectory garden.

Half the passengers saved
and half are buried.

*

Irène

And when the tide changed
it was water turning
in a salty womb.

We rolled under and over,
every body raised and scattered,
shelved onto the beach
or bobbed into the harbour's arm
or thrown up on a slip.

The men were collected,
lined up like timber on the pier,
coffin-boxed and buried.

And me? Did the sea
make mermaid with my hair,
strip me of my whore's lace,
cast me anew?

No. Enough of your stories.

I was a woman drowned,
washed up on the shore.

*

Small Boat Fisherman

Sometimes it's like the wrecks
are sucking at your boat
as you pass over.

We'll be crossing Danger Passage
past Les Grunes Vaudin
and there's a wobble on the radio
fibrillations, always in the same spot.

Not that I believe in ghosts
just the engine and my pots
– spiders, *chancres*, lobsters –
my right to make a living.

Since Viking times they've been
wrecking themselves on this coast.
The sea bed's mostly rock and reef –
the whole island doubles in size
on a low tide
        think of all the lives
shucked out on these *rocques* and *cricqs,*
stakks and *etacs,*
this lone *equervière.*

I could go on –
each rock is named on the chart
the wrecks too.

Sometimes we'll drift into a patch –
the boat feels altered
        everything is still
breeze   water   mackerel in buckets

and I'm holding my breath

till she creaks and groans
and we're round the headland
out into the bay.

chancre brown crab; *rocque* rock; *cricq* crevice in a rock; *stakk* high
pyramid shaped rock; *etac* high rock; *equervière* rock frequented by
cormorants

HEDY AND DOROTHEA

From November 1943 until May 1945, Dorothea Weber, née Le Brocq, hid Jewish woman Hedwig Bercu in her house at 7 West Park Avenue, St Helier, Jersey.

All we have are fragments of their story:

a pile of Hedy's clothes
folded neatly on the sand
to fake her suicide;

night-time forays
to the beach for food;

a pig slaughtered in the bathroom,
every edible piece consumed.

A typist of no nationality
stated the Wanted notice
in the evening paper.

I stare at Dorothea's eyes
in the photo on her registration card
and she looks back in defiance.

What did they do all day,
these two friends of unclear origin?
Did they bicker?
Did their cycles coincide?

Here in this icing sugar street
at least one set of neighbours knew
and brought crushed aspirin
when Hedy was unwell.

Their house still stands
trim in freshly painted stucco,
a gold-leaf number seven
faded in the fanlight.

I want to open the house up at its hinge
and find them through the hungry
gloom of the hall, Dorothea
putting a kettle on the stove,
Hedy reading in a wicker chair.

But their story is one
they both want to lose;
forgetting is harder than hiding.

And when it is over
they lock the front door,
disappear off the page
in their post-war shoes.

7 WEST PARK AVENUE

The house is a bell, is a shell snapped shut
is a box with a lid and the lid locked up

is a pocket, is a pouch with the cord pulled tight
is a well with steps treading down from the light.

The house is a whisper, a shrug on the street
the placing on floorboards of soft-slippered feet

is a hole, a cellar, a bookcase on a hinge
is the view from an attic
                     – daylight of seagulls –
                         is salt in the wind.

The house is a puzzle, a trick or a chance
movement at a window, the risk of a glance.

The house is a pebble, a ripple on water.
When you walk by, it is stucco, bricks, mortar.

A SEA FOG

Her ghost
takes me by the hand,
leads me down the lane
in fog to school.
In my dream she stoops,
little old lady
she never became,
dead in her fifties, though
old enough at five to see
hunger in the labourers'
eyes, their rags
brown as leaf mould.
She had green
remembering eyes,
showed me
colours and patterns
in a hedge,
the stippled universe
in a piece of shell.
When the fog lifts,
she says, you can still
taste it on your tongue.

SLOWLY, WE DISMANTLE THE HUTS

When the camps are abandoned, the workers shipped away, we take some of the wood, the boards from the huts, the planks where they slept, and use it to burn on our household fires that last siege winter of the war. Later, we use it to make sheds in our gardens, hen houses, a bench. We put up shelves in our barns. Or we burn the wood there and then just to get rid of it. I'm just telling you what we did with the wood, the boards from the huts, the planks where they slept, and why we do not want to think about it anymore, about the wood, because it is still there in our sheds and our gardens, in the shelves of our barns. We have taken the wood into our homes. We have burned it on our fires.

THIS AND OTHER WARTIME STORIES

He is out after curfew time, jumps behind the hedge when he
hears the Germans driving down the lane, headlights silvering the
trees.

He bears his body low because the hedge is only as high as a sack
of grain, the interrogation room at Silvertide a short drive away,
then the boat to a prison in France.

He must keep still, but his breathing is so loud his whole frame
shakes, and then he hears another body breathing beside him in
the muddy leaves and grass, their startled eyes meet and then fear
turns to relief as he recognises the face in the moonlight as that of
his neighbour
                 or a boy he was at school with,
                      or a man he once sat next to on the bus

because every family has this story to tell, an uncle or father,
cousin or friend, still lying wretched in the ditch behind the hedge,
suspended in the moment before the car of German soldiers drives
off.

The story tumbles out of their drawstring bag of tales like the last
precious coal, and they pass it down the decades, this and other
wartime stories, fragile yet burning, their faces lit as they tell each
other, the only people who already know.

MEADOW BANK

German Underground Hospital, St Lawrence

You are scared to talk about it
the smell of cordite in the tunnel
as you and Oswald tumbled inside
through a crack and walk among bodies.

Sleeping, Oswald said. He could hear them breathing.
You heard nothing with your glue ears.

Your sister raises her eyes.
Your brother says you're making it up –
little brother, born the last fierce
winter of the war, a bundle passed between women,
knowing only sleep and milk and women's arms.

Another time, skirmishing high up on the bank
above the labour camp, you and Oswald saw
wooden boxes roughly made, with bodies in face down.

You were ten. Now at eighty-three you whisper,
hiding what you say from your brother
and sister, *Take this down, I want to tell it now.*

MURATTI CAP

Match final – 4 May 1939

She takes out his cap, sunken, flat
empty on her lap and strokes
the folds of shadowy navy
the bee-gold tassel; cold wonder
at the afterlife an object has
pitching her back to a bold spring day
young men in friendly battle
their lives set out before them
like an astonishing trick.

ESCAPE AT NIGHT

She longed for the prairies and desert lands
of the 1930s rolling endlessly on screen
at The Forum, a ribbon of road unravelling
behind her eyelids, the vista-rush of opportunity.

He wanted borders, edges finitely drawn,
boundaries you couldn't overspill, knowing
if you were lost you'd bump against
the island's salty margins, find your way home.

And when the time came to escape at night –
a boat, five friends, a basket of provisions –
he helped them drag the hidden dinghy
from barn to shore and out onto the sea

ticking with mines below them,
and wretched, watched her boat get smaller,
as he tidied up the tins and wrappers
of their final meal together.

TEN DAYS

This poem draws substantially from the 1946 BBC radio play written by Leonard Cottrell based on Jerseyman Harold Le Druillenec's experiences in Bergen-Belsen during the last ten days before the camp was liberated by British forces in April 1945.

He has two friends.
On the second day they find a long brick hut
stacked neatly with the dead.

Their own hut is made of wood and packed
with starving men like them.
Like them. What are they like, now?

At dawn, those who cannot drag themselves
out of the hut for roll call
are put with the dead.

On the third day more convoys of men arrive.
On the fourth day more convoys of men arrive.
On the fifth day more convoys of men arrive

And on the sixth, the men are made
to drag the dead to burial pits
using strips of blanket tied to ankles.

On the seventh day they are filling a fourth pit.

On the eighth day one of the friends dies.

On the ninth day they hide under a blanket
but the guards beat them back to work.

On the tenth day his friend finds
fresh grass to eat outside one of the huts.

Then gunshots, explosions,
the camp gates are opened.

He weighs ninety pounds.

When he sees himself
in the mirror for the first time
he looks behind to see who is there.

VIEW FROM THE BACK GARDEN OF THE MILITARY PRISON

Newgate Street Prison, Jersey

Lucy, lovely lady, in the cell next to mine
asks, do I remember the child refugees
who were coming to Jersey before the war?
She and her sister Susanne were to take in two.

I did remember. The fuss and hullabaloo.
Some high-up people not wanting foreigners,
however young, on our island. The fourteen
Kindertransport children did not come.

A child myself in 1939, I'd felt the blister-prick
of shame for the first time, spreading through me
like a sudden rash, and I told her this as we stood
in the prison yard, days before the war's end.

Lucy, lovely lady, took me by the hands,
kissed my cheek, tears in her eyes.

A GERMAN SOLDIER GUARDING THE ATLANTIC WALL

D-Day, 6 June 1944 – Liberation, 9 May 1945
A section of the Atlantic Wall, St Ouen's Bay, Jersey

At first we tried to count the planes
flying over the island from England to France
but there were too many, so we listened instead
to the Yankee pilots on our walkie-talkie –
untangling their sun-tanned voices
from the airwaves' crackle.

Thank God we were here,
in a sandy dug-out on the island,
not getting killed in France.
Even being on guard at night was a reverie –
the air soft, lullaby sigh of the sea.
On a full moon the whole bay lit up silver
from L'Oeillier to L'Etacquerel.

By September, St Malo had fallen.
Orders came reminding us to 'heil' Hitler.
Invasion wasn't coming to these islands.
Cut off from Germany, cut off from France,
all we knew was gorse, sand, rocks, saltwater.
We'd long ago stopped listening to orders.

Then hunger came among us, controlled everything.
No exercises, discipline, drill. Rations reduced
to bread and turnips. An order came
to chew every mouthful thirty times.

We found limpets on the rocks
between La Rocco and Corbière,
cooked them thoroughly on small fires

at the beach, but as weeks passed
we ate them where we found them,
raw from the hard tent of their shell.

When fuel ran out we burned driftwood,
seaweed, railway sleepers,
our own invasion posts from the beach.
The clever ones started to learn English.

We all wanted it to end, and when it did
we let off tracer ammunition all along the coast.
We marched into captivity across the sand,
up rope ladders hanging from the sides of ships
into cabins well below the waterline.

They gave us white bread, and corned beef from a tin.
For twelve years we'd had bad times.
Now life was getting better.

DANCING ON THE ATLANTIC WALL

D-Day, 6 June 1944 – Liberation, 9 May 1945
A section of the Atlantic Wall, St Brelade's Bay, Jersey

That summer we lay side by side at night,
too scared to talk, planes roaring overhead

on their way to France,
the sky lit up with star shells.

Flash and *boom* went the guns.
Putty fell from our windowpanes.

By day the American bombers flew so low
we could see the navigators' heads

as we stood on the stretch of Atlantic Wall
marking the end of our garden.

Autumn came. We saw stranded German sailors
gleaning the empty wheat fields.

Our parents hunched over the nest
of their crystal radio,

searching the static for news –
France was free. No one coming for us.

Winter tides battered the wall, left seaweed
in our garden. We took our bowls

to the communal kitchen, collected twigs
in the stripped-out shell of our old pram.

No flour, no fuel, no candles. Our parents stepped
out of their selves and into their hunger.

We burned yellow gorse in the grate, woke
in the blue light of dawn, our stomachs aching.

And when it was all of a sudden over –
the well-fed men in uniforms

posing for the camera, fountain pens in their hands –
we danced on our wall at the end of the garden,

arms raised silly as statues, bodies dry as driftwood;
we were gold, we were silver, we were sand.

PHOTOGRAPH OF A SERGEANT IN THE MOROCCAN TIRAILLEUR REGIMENT

'We have been very miserable at times, but the help
and the interest of which you gave us testimony
rendered our prisoner life less miserable.'

Sergeant Mohamed ben Mohamed
6 June 1945, Letter to the *Evening Post*

He is sitting very upright
on the bentwood chair
in the camp's tidy kitchen,
wild flowers in a tin on the table.

He is sitting very upright,
wearing the leather
plaited sandals
of a colonial uniform.

It is strictly forbidden
for members of the North African
Contingent to wear civilian clothes
in the town
                states a note to the camp
from the Liberating Forces.

He is sitting very upright,
staring at the camera,
at the photographer
                Monsieur Dubras,
businessman, parfumier,
retired French lieutenant,
tireless smuggler of provisions
for the sergeant and his men.

pommes de terre, oignons
pantalons, chaussettes

Reservoirs of men.

He is sitting very upright
on the bentwood chair
in the camp's tidy kitchen.

He is staring at the camera.
He is staring at us.

AND ALL THE WORLD IS REDEEMED

Christmas Eve, 1947.
The Sally Army Band
plays carols in the Royal Square.
The gentle notes of Silent Night
shimmer up from trumpet, cornet,
tenor horn with their doll's house
clip-on music stands. Tinsel
scatter scratch of the snare drum.
The uniformed bosoms
of the singers rise and fall
as notes float effortlessly
down King Street
to shoppers browsing
Woolworths, Burtons,
Boudin's Bikes,
the iced cake spectaculars
in Gaudin's bay window.
Bouan Noué, Bouan Noué,
and Mr Le Druillenec stands
stock still rigid
gripping his nephew's arm,
hearing, hearing
   Stille nacht, heilige nacht,
   Alles schläft, einsam wacht
the concentration camp choir,
roll call in the dark,
three years ago now.

Bouan Noué Happy Christmas

POLITICAL PRISONER

A list of Channel Islanders who died in camps, requested by the Home Office in 1959, is jotted on a scrap of paper attached to the Bailiff's reply. Inaccurate, incomplete, the list is partially obscured, states the book I am reading, by a tear. Not tear as in drop, indicating sadness, but tear as in rent, a small rip on a snippet of paper which is itself an afterthought.

Their crimes were listening to the news, typing news-sheets, sheltering escaped prisoners or stealing food. Their crimes were espionage or owning a camera, slapping an officer as he groped your thigh or assaulted your mother.

Crimes for which they died at Ravensbrück and Flossenburg, Cherche-Midi and Zoeschen, Frankfurt, Straubing, Hamelin and other places arrived at by railway tracks laddering the fields of Europe.

NO ROOM TO EXPLAIN

The space on the compensation form
was only three lines long –
no room to explain

why the projectionist,
putting on films for tourists in town,
changes the reels with hands
and nails that are clawed

or why a son's only memory
of his father
is playing hide and seek
among *vraic* heaps
on the beach

or why a mother,
sweeping the cobbles
or weeding a patch,
turns to her neighbour and says,
My Sidney will do this when he gets home.

vraic seaweed

POUQUELAYE

Our elders sung stories
to help us sleep, conjuring
the comfort of firelight
with their song.
They led us down *pouquelayes*,
fairy stepping stones
yellow with lichen,
cushioned in moss.
They held our hands
in the granite chambers,
scented with the sea.
Other children were not so lucky.
Ch't ch't mot. Ch't ch't mot.
They tucked us under candlewick
and closed our eyes.
Tchi pitchi. Tchi pitchi.
We lost our hold, we fell asleep.

pouquelaye prehistoric burial site or stones of the fairies; *ch't ch't mot*
hush; *tchi pitchi* what a pity

DESCRIBING GRANITE

A rosy speckled heat emanates from granite walls,
not the grey granite of colder places to the North
but pink and sparkling –
a faceted sharpness under the touch,
freckled with grains of igneous light,
from red to orange, brown to bruise,
and shawled with a yellow pulse of lichen.
Pink of the vernacular farmhouse,
marriage stone lintel, cider press.
Pink of the *pauvre* stones in the *brecque*,
the dolmen, *pouquelaye* – rough-hewn, unpolished.
The finest orangey pinks came from Mont Mado,
crystallised with tiny seeds of red and brown,
cornered and nosed into shape by quarrymen
who had a feel for the rock,
steel tools sharpened in the fire.
There are moon-pocked reefs at La Rocque,
magnificent behemoths of soil-dark stone,
trimmed with waterfalls of milky quartz;
giant table slabs at Gorey,
chequered with feldspar and barnacle.
People clamber and trip over rock pool and boulder
at Corbière, searching for bands of red
revealed on an ebbing tide, content,
as when walking on sand
you stoop to pick up a pebble,
balance its pleasing weight in your palm,
its perfect human scale, whoever you are,
howsoever you came to be there,
enamoured with granite's shifting lustre,
wanting to write it down –
all this light.

pauvre stones stones marking a field, the rental income of which went to the poor; *brecque* gap, field entrance; *pouquelaye* prehistoric burial site or stones of the fairies

PHOTOGRAPHS

Harold Le Druillenec, Identity Card photograph

Hyam Goldman, Identity Card photograph

Dorothea Weber, née Le Brocq, Identity Card photograph

Hedy Bercu, Alien Registration Card photograph

Mohamed ben Mohamed

Photographs reproduced
courtesy of Jersey Heritage

NOTES

A Sapper's Tale
This poem uses sapper Bill Harvey's account on the BBC's People's War website
https://www.bbc.co.uk/history/ww2peopleswar/stories/17/a419521
7.shtml

The evacuation of allied forces and civilians from western France from 15 to 25 June 1940 followed the evacuation of Dunkirk earlier that month. Small boats from Jersey assisted in the evacuation of St Malo just days before Jersey was itself occupied by the German forces.

Whatever Else Is Wrong, It's Been a Beautiful Day
The words of the title were allegedly spoken by a Guernsey politician to calm an anxious crowd minutes before the island was bombed.

La Soupe d'Andgulle
Conger Eel Soup is a Jersey speciality and is traditionally garnished with marigold petals.

Beehive Stores
Hyam Goldman was a British national who had been resident in Jersey for 32 years at the start of the Occupation. It is thought that he was not deported and his shop and apiary were allowed to remain open, despite the Nazi Aryanisation of businesses on the island, because the German authorities required his skills as a beekeeper due to the sugar shortage and for the medicinal uses of the honey. Goldman never recovered from his experiences during the Occupation and on 10 October 1950 he committed suicide. His story is recounted in *The Jews in the Channel Islands during the German Occupation 1940-1945*, by Frederick Cohen (2000).

Arrival of the Slave Workers
As in other occupied countries, the Organisation Todt was in charge of slave and forced labour camps in the Channel Islands. Sixteen thousand men were brought to the islands to build

fortifications which were part of the Atlantic Wall. Workers were conscripted from across Europe and Russia, and included Spanish Republicans, North Africans, Poles, Czechs, and men, women and children from Ukraine and other parts of the Soviet Union.

Potato, Flour
This poem draws on Nan Le Ruez' *Jersey Occupation Diary* (1994).

The Sand-Gathering Railway
'… it was estimated that the OT [Organisation Todt] removed over one million tons of sand from Grouville Bay and its gritty appearance can be seen in practically every concrete structure erected by the Germans in Jersey.' *The Organisation Todt and the Fortress Engineers in the Channel Islands*, Michael Ginns (2004).

No Hinterland
This poem includes the testimony of Lager Sylt slave workers from Russia, Ukraine, Poland and Spain – Kirill Nevrov, Georgi Kondakov, Ted Misiewicz and John Dlamau. Document compiled by Olga Finch for the Forced Workers Memorial at La Hougue Bie Museum, Jersey Heritage.

Tins and Jars
Let 'em starve, Winston Churchill, 27 September 1944. A handwritten note at the end of the minutes of a cabinet meeting. The full quote is '*Let 'em starve. No fighting. They can rot at their leisure*'. Presumably, Churchill was referring to the German garrison but the effects were also felt by Channel Islanders.

Listening Party
Harold Le Druillenec, his sisters Louisa Gould and Ivy Forster and several friends were sentenced for sheltering an escaped Russian worker and for listening to the radio news. Louisa died at Ravensbrück concentration camp on 13 February 1945. Harold was the only Briton still left alive at Bergen-Belsen concentration camp at its liberation. See www.frankfallaarchive.org.

Hedy and Dorothea
Both women survived the war. The story is recounted in *The Jews in the Channel Islands during the German Occupation 1940-1945,* Frederick Cohen (2000). Dorothea was posthumously awarded the honour of 'Righteous Among Nations' by Yad Vashem in 2016 and was made a British Hero of the Holocaust in 2018. The ceremonies were attended by descendants of both women.

'post-war shoes': after Sarah Kirsch

Muratti Cap
The Muratti is an annual football competition held in the Channel Islands.

Escape at Night
Of the 152 men and women who attempted to escape by boat from Jersey, 34 were captured or drowned and 118 reached the safety of the English or, after August 1944, the French coast.

Ten Days
See note to Listening Party

See 'The Man from Belsen', in *BBC Features,* Leonard Cottrell (1950)

View from the Back Garden of the Military Prison
The title comes from a drawing by Susanne Malherbe (also known as Marcel Moore) of the view seen through the keyhole of her cell in Newgate Street Prison, Jersey. See *Any Day Now,* Wendy Tipping (2015). The encounter in the poem between Lucy Schwob (also known as Claude Cahun) and Joe Mière is recounted in *Never to be Forgotten,* Joe Mière (2004).

Susanne and Lucy were French artists living in Jersey and sentenced for resistance activities.

A German Soldier Guarding the Atlantic Wall
The poem is based on an account of the last days of the war by Herr Georg Brefka in CIOR NO.23.

Photograph of a Sergeant in the Moroccan Tirailleur Regiment
There were 115 North African prisoners of war in Jersey from Algeria, Morocco and Tunisia. Many had been taken prisoner by the Germans in 1940 after the occupation of France. They were sent to Jersey as part of the labour force and were helped considerably by the local population, especially those from the French community. See Margaret Ginns' article and research papers, Jersey Heritage archives, L/D/25/A/24.

'reservoir of men': a phrase used by French Lieutenant Colonel Mangin, a leading proponent of the idea of empire as a source of limitless manpower for European wars.

Political Prisoner
'Bailiff': the President of the States of Jersey

No Room to Explain
This poem draws on the following sources: *The Ultimate Sacrifice,* Paul Sanders (2004), *Islands in Danger,* Alan and Mary Wood (1955), The Frank Falla Archive, www.frankfallaarchive.org.

The book I am reading: *Victims of Nazi Persecution in the Channel Islands*, Gilly Carr (2019)

*

In addition to the sources already listed, the following books were invaluable in researching this book: *The Model Occupation,* Madeleine Bunting (2004 edition); *The British Channel Islands Under German Occupation 1940-45*, Paul Sanders (2005); *Protest, Defiance and Resistance in the Channel Islands*, Gilly Carr, Paul Sanders and Louise Willmot (2014); *On British Soil, Nazi Persecution in the Channel Islands*, Gilly Carr (2017); *Jersey Occupation Diary*, Nan Le

Ruez (1994); *The Occupation of Jersey Day by Day, The Personal Diary of Senator Edward Le Quesne*, Edward Le Quesne (1999); and *Jersey Place Names Volumes I and II*, Joan and Charles Stevens and Jean Arthur (1985).

ACKNOWLEDGMENTS

Emptying the Egg of Its Song was first published in *The Moth*. *Beehive Stores, Soap Hoard* and *Foreign Worker* were first published in *Envoi*. *Open Day at the Observatory* and a version of *Photograph of a Sergeant in the Moroccan Tirailleur Regiment* and *The Wreck of the Schokland* were first published in *The High Window*. *Hedy and Dorothea* and *7 West Park Avenue* were read at the ceremony bestowing the honour of Righteous Among Nations on Dorothea Weber. *Muratti Cap* was commissioned by Jersey Heritage for the Literary Labels exhibition.

Thanks are due to Art House Jersey for awarding me a grant to research and write this book.

Thanks are also due to Lucy Layton, Jane Menczer, Dr Gilly Carr and Pippa Le Quesne for their help and encouragement right from the start, Tamar Yoseloff and the Wednesday seminar group, and Philip Gross for his advice and understanding at various different points along the book's way. Thank you to Gary Font and Robert Le Sueur and the staff at Jersey Archive. Thank you also to Paul Aked and Frank Le Blancq from the Meteorological Section of the Jersey Department of the Environment for showing me around the extraordinary Maison St Louis Observatory complete with Father Rey's duffle coat and beret still hanging on the door. Thank you to Ed Scott for lending me his hardcover editions of *Jersey Place Names* and to Amal Camargo for conversations about Mohamed ben Mohamed's letter and handwriting. I'd like to thank my mother's sisters and brothers (and especially Kathleen) for their stories and memories, and my sister Rebecca for her enthusiasm and support. My greatest thanks go to Alex for his keen editorial eye and his faith in the project right from the beginning, and to Lily and Clara who have lived with the presence of this book in our home for a large proportion of their lives.

THE HIGH WINDOW

The following collections are also available from our website,
where further information will be found:
https://thehighwindowpress.com/the-press/

A Slow Blues, New and Selected Poems by David Cooke
Angles & Visions by Anthony Costello
The Emigrant's Farewell by James W. Wood
Four American Poets edited by Anthony Costello
Dust by Bethany W. Pope
From Inside by Anthony Howell
The Edge of Seeing by John Duffy
End Phrase by Mario Susko
Bloody, proud and murderous men, adulterers and enemies of God
by Steve Ely
Bare Bones by Norton Hodges
Wounded Light by James Russell
Bone Antler Stone by Tim Miller
Wardrobe Blues for a Japanese Lady by Alan Price
Trodden Before by Patricia McCarthy
Janky Tuk Tuks by Wendy Holborow
Cradle of Bones by Frances Sackett
Of Course, the Yellow Cab by Ken Champion
Forms of Exile: Selected Poems of Marina Tsvetaeva
trans. by Belinda Cooke
West South North North South East by Daniel Bennett
Surfaces by Michael Lesher
Man Walking on Water with Tie Askew by Margaret Wilmot
Songs of Realisation by Anthony Howell
Building a Kingdom, New and Selected Poems 1989-2019
by James W. Wood

The Unmaking by Tim O'Leary
Out of the Blue, Selected Poems by Wendy Klein
Man at the Ice House by Alison Mace
Empire of Eden by Tom Laichas